# Badass

## WOMEN
## OF
## THE BIBLE

# Table of Contents

# From the Author

*I*n 2017 I taught the last series of Bible studies I would teach at a Dallas faith-based nonprofit where I had to worked as Director of Spiritual Support for a little over 14 years. The title of the series was Badass Biblical Women.

Each Thursday evening from 6:00p.m. to 8:30p.m. women who had been prostituted, sexually exploited and had experienced sexual trauma and addiction, would make their way from school or work to have dinner together and experience a Womanist biblical interpretation of texts detailing narratives of women in Scripture.

In these classes we read and discussed the stories of Sarah, Hagar, Shiphrah, Puah, the Shulamite woman, and the key women in Moses life.

Over the years I had also taught Bible studies on Eve, Sheerah, Rahab, The Daughters of Zelophehad, Delilah, the Syrophoenecian Woman and her Daughter, The hemorrhaging woman, the bent over woman, Perpetua and Felicitus (extra biblical women), Queen Vashti, Hannah and Penninah and many others.

Teaching the Bible with these particular women helped me learn in a very practical way the importance of a womanist biblical hermeneutic.

Although I rarely used the term womanist hermeneutic in those classes, the women knew there was something different about what they were learning. They understood quite clearly that something transformative, something revolutionary, something that would help them navigate the patriarchal world in which they lived was transpiring.

I will forever be grateful for those Thursday night classes that paved the way for this book.

Typically, the narratives detailing the lives and experiences of biblical women are written from the perspective of the male gaze. They are in service to or part of, a larger male-centered narrative and more are often than not, misrepresented and misinterpreted reflecting a patriarchal and misogynist culture. The stories of biblical women we most often hear place them in subordinate and un-empowered positions, failing to take into account their agency and self-derived survival strategies made necessary by the patriarchal culture in which they were forced to live. Rarely are the stories of biblical women the focus of preaching.

This Bible Study Series, which includes sample sermons, elevates and centers the narratives of biblical women. These are women who either directly or indirectly, like the hundreds of women I've ministered to and served over the years, experienced some kind of emotional distress. The sermons highlight biblical women who despite their challenges, found a way to navigate life in ways that enabled their own flourishing as well as that of the larger community.

As you read and engage this study, I encourage you to mine these stories for womanist tenets of traditional communalism (community wholeness), radical subjectivity (she matters), redemptive self-love (loving oneself regardless), and critical engagement (confronting the Powers).

—Dr. Irie Lynne Session

# Key Terms

**<u>Biblical Exegesis</u>** is a theological term used to describe an approach to interpreting a passage in the Bible by critical analysis. Responsible exegesis includes using the context around the passage, comparing it with other parts of the Bible, and applying an understanding of the language and customs of the time of the writing in an attempt to understand clearly what the original writer intended to convey. In other words, it is trying to "pull out" of the passage the meaning inherent in it.

**<u>Eisegesis</u>** is the opposite of exegesis and is a person's particular interpretation of scriptures that are not evident in the text itself. In other words, Eisegesis is "putting into" the passage a preconceived idea, theme, and personal perspective not apparent in the text.

**<u>Biblical Hermeneutics</u>** is the study of the theory and practice of interpretation concerning the books of the Bible. A hermeneutic is a particular lens through which one views and interprets a biblical text. Everyone who interprets the Bible for preaching, teaching, or personal study does so by using a particular hermeneutic; even if they are unaware of what it is. Dr. Irie's method of biblical interpretation is womanism.

**<u>Hermeneutic of Suspicion</u>** is employed by womanist's in reinterpreting biblical texts that have been used to oppress, marginalize, and subordinate women and other ethnic and sexual minorities. Use of a hermeneutic of suspicion suggests the way the text has been interpreted is death-dealing rather than life-giving. In other words, it's a lie.

**<u>Pericope</u>** - a unit of scripture in the Bible; a section or a passage with a beginning and an end.

**Womanism** is described by New Testament Womanist Biblical Scholar Mitzi J. Smith as "sister to feminism and not her child."[1] Womanism, unlike feminism is centered in the lived experiences of Black women. Black women live at the intersection of race, gender, and class oppression and therefore, as persons society has marginalized, have an epistemological advantage—a way of seeing injustice and creating solutions for it that benefit entire communities, not just Black women.

**Patriarchy**, according to black feminist author and cultural critic bell hooks, is "a political-social system that insists males are inherently dominating, superior to everything and everyone deemed weak, especially females, and endowed with the right to dominate and rule over the weak and to maintain that dominance through various forms of psychological terrorism and violence."[2]

1       Mitzi J. Smith, *Womanist Sass and Talk Back: Social (In)Justice, Intersectionality, and Biblical Interpretation* (Oregon, Cascade Books, 2018), chap. 3, Kindle.
2       "Patriarchy," bell hooks, *No Borders*, accessed May 8, 2019, https://imaginenoborders.org/pdf/zines/UnderstandingPatriarchy.pdf.

# Chapter One

## Joshua 2:1–21

*T*hen Joshua son of Nun sent two men secretly from Shittim as spies, saying, "Go, view the land, especially Jericho." So they went, and entered the house of a prostitute whose name was Rahab, and spent the night there. **2** The king of Jericho was told, "Some Israelites have come here tonight to search out the land." **3** Then the king of Jericho sent orders to Rahab, "Bring out the men who have come to you, who entered your house, for they have come only to search out the whole land."

**4** But the woman took the two men and hid them. Then she said, "True, the men came to me, but I did not know where they came from. **5** And when it was time to close the gate at dark, the men went out. Where the men went, I do not know. Pursue them quickly, for you can overtake them." **6** She had, however, brought them up to the roof and hidden them with the stalks of flax that she had laid out on the roof. **7** So the men pursued them on the way to the Jordan as far as the fords. As soon as the pursuers had gone out, the gate was shut. **8** Before they went to sleep, she came up to them on the roof **9** and said to the men: "I know that the LORD has given you the land, and that dread of you has fallen on us, and that all the inhabitants of the land melt in fear before you. **10** For we have heard how the LORD dried up the water of the Red Sea before you when you came out of Egypt, and what you did to the two kings of the Amorites that were beyond the Jordan, to Sihon and Og, whom you utterly destroyed. **11** As soon as we heard it, our hearts melted, and there was no courage left in any of us because of you. The LORD your God is indeed God in heaven above and on earth below. **12** Now then, since I have dealt kindly with you, swear to me by the LORD that you in turn will deal kindly with my family. Give me a sign of good faith **13** that you will spare my father and mother, my brothers and sisters, and all who belong to them, and deliver our lives from death."

**14** The men said to her, "Our life for yours! If you do not tell this business of ours, then we will deal kindly and faithfully with you when the LORD gives us the land." **15** Then she let them down by a rope through the window, for her house was on the outer side of the city wall and she resided within the wall itself. **16** She said to them, "Go toward the hill country, so that the pursuers may not come upon you. Hide yourselves there three days, until the pursuers have returned; then afterward you may go your way."

**17** The men said to her, "We will be released from this oath that you have made us swear to you **18** if we invade the land and you do not tie this crimson cord in the window through which you let us down, and you do not gather into your house your father and mother, your brothers, and all your family. **19** If any of you go out of the doors of your house into the street, they shall be responsible for their own death, and we shall be innocent; but if a hand is laid upon any who are with you in the house, we shall bear the responsibility for their death. **20** But if you tell this business of ours, then we shall be released from this oath that you made us swear to you." **21** She said, "According to your words, so be it." She sent them away and they departed. Then she tied the crimson cord in the window.

# What You May Not Know

- Joshua, after the death of Moses, succeeded him as leader of the Israelite community.

- Jericho was the first Canaanite city attacked by the Israelites upon their entry into Canaan.

- To dismantle the patriarchal practice of demonizing women who men buy for their sexual pleasure, I will use the term prostituted rather than prostitute.

- The language of prostituted holds accountable and problematizes men who are buyers of sex.

# Questions for Theological Reflection

1. Describe Rahab's character. What were her values? What was important to her?

2. What was her motivation for helping the spies?

3. What did she risk?

4. What motivates you?

5. What are you willing to risk in order to have the life you want?

6. What was the significance of the crimson cord?

7. What symbols reflect your vision for your life?

# Rahab: Prostituted, Pragmatic & Partnered with God

## Introduction

What happens when people live with their backs against the wall? That is, when society is structured in a manner that affords them few viable options to earn a living wage to care for themselves and their families? How do we judge such people in light of their real lived experiences? Well, a womanist interpretation of Rahab does just that. A Womanist reading focuses on Rahab as a woman whose back was against the wall, every single day; a woman who was also responsible for and in charge of providing for herself and her family.

## Rahab: A Prostituted Woman

Rahab's back was so far against the wide Jericho wall that she made her home in it. The Bible says she lived inside the city wall. Living in the wall meant marginalization. A home in the wall was living with a sense of hopelessness. Rahab was stuck. Stuck in a life she never planned for herself. She was stuck in a situation of degradation, waking up morning by morning to the touch of another musty man who would get up and go home to his wife, leaving a few dollars on the nightstand. In contemporary society, Rahab's sisters do the same thing—retrieve money from a nightstand in order to buy groceries for their children, all the while feeling worthless because this transaction is a reminder that their backs are still up against the wall.

Rahab was prostituted. I used the term prostituted intentionally to highlight those who transact business on the bodies of women and girls. Specifically, men who buy women for sex. Sometimes a place to live is the currency that is exchanged. Other times, money or food. What is clear is that Rahab was prostituted. This is an important re-reading of this Joshua passage because few preachers highlight the spies as johns, and thus pro-curers of sex from women. Granted, the two spies were on a mission of espionage, but they also stopped at a brothel, a stop they were never instructed to make.

The sexual proclivities of the spies, at least for the typical church-goer, remain invisible, primarily because few preachers interpret the text in such a way as to expose their conflicting behavior. Men on a mission from God and men who spent the night in a brothel. The Common English Bible uses the phrase, "they bedded down there." The literal translation is "they lay there." Hebrew Bible Scholar, Dr. Wil Gafney in her sermon on Rahab, "Who You Calling a Whore,"[3] sheds additional light on the verb "to lay." Gafney determined the verb "sh-k-v" means to lie down for sleep and sexual intercourse. However, the typical explanation by most preachers for the spies seemingly unusual stop was that brothels were the best place to secure information.

But a close reading of the passage reveals the spies never asked Rahab any questions about the goings on in the city. It seems to me if their reason for hitting up a brothel was to gain information, the author of the book of Joshua would have noted at least one question asked by the spies. Don't you think? Isn't it interesting how we seek to justify the behavior of the spies? The truth is, men buy sex from women. Even religious men. Even men who go to church. Even men on a mission from God.

Although the Joshua text gives little socioeconomic data on Rahab, a case can nonetheless be made, that she had few marketable skills with which to make a conventional living; prostituted women in antiquity were on the lowliest economic and social rung. They "were not the respectable and accepted members of society in most cases, they were slaves or freed women without other means of supporting themselves."[4] In the 21st Century prostitution is a regular occurrence in urban patriarchal societies. Prostitution flourishes wherever there is an unequal distribution of

---

3        "Remixed Gospel of Rahab: Who Are You Calling a Whore," Wil Gafney Blog, accessed May 8, 2019, https://www.wilgafney.com/tag/rahab/.
4        Thomas A.J. McGinn, *The Economy of Prostitution in the Roman World: A Study of Social History and the Brothel* (Ann Arbor: University of Michigan Press, 2004), 60
.

power and status and where sex roles are hierarchical placing women at the bottom. Rahab, a woman at the bottom of social, economic, and gender hierarchies had limited choices.

**Rahab was Pragmatic**

I use the word choice here, loosely. What do people do who have to make choices that are not really choices? A patriarchal culture placed Rahab in a position where being prostituted became a survival strategy for she and her family. So, Rahab was pragmatic. She was practical. Given her situation in life, the patriarchal culture in which she lived, and lack of economic and financial resources, she had to make a choice not really a choice. Each and every day all over the world women are forced to consider a choice that's not really a choice. Turn a trick to pay rent or face eviction? Trade sex to feed their children or they go hungry. A choice not a choice. I know, some of you can't imagine this kind of conundrum. But my work with hundreds of women testifies, it's real.

**Sex Trafficking and LGBTQ Youth**

But cis-gender women and girls are not the only ones forced to make a choice that's not a choice. They're not the only group of pragmatists. Prostituted youth also have their backs against the wall.

Here's what I mean. In certain circumstances prostitution is also a form of sex trafficking. And while sex trafficking:

"affects all demographics, traffickers commonly target individuals who lack strong support networks, are facing financial strains, have experienced violence in the past, or who are marginalized by society. Without adequate community support, youth who identify as lesbian, gay, bisexual, transgender, queer, or questioning (LGBTQ) are at particular risk for sex trafficking. Homeless youth are disproportionately vulnerable to being prostituted. Homeless youth are often forced to make a choice not a choice. Research shows up to 40% of homeless youth identify as LGBTQ. Of these: 46% ran away because of family rejection; 7.4x's more likely to experience acts of sexual violence than their heterosexual peers; 3–7x's more likely to engage in survival sex to meet basic needs, such as shelter, food, drugs, and toiletries."[5]

The news is even more alarming. LGBTQ youth face higher rates of discrimination, violence, and economic instability than their non-LGBTQ peers.

Like Rahab, LGBTQ youth live with their backs against the wall. And because they are faced with fewer resources, employment opportunities, or social supports, LGBTQ youth who are away from home must find ways to meet their basic needs and may therefore enter the street economy, engaging in commercial sex to meet these needs. LGBTQ are prostituted as a means of survival.

## Rahab Partnered with God

But even when a person's back is against a wall they still have worth. We live in a world that creates structures and systems that push certain people to the wall. It is those structures and oppressive systems that must be dismantled and eradicated. It is the systems that create injustice that must be eliminated, not the people oppressed by those systems. The people have worth and value, the systems do not.

Rahab was prostituted and forced to make a pragmatic choice not a choice, because she lived in a patriarchal society. But even in that system, God was able to connect and partner with Rahab. Although life had placed her back against a wall of poverty, she had a sense of value. I know she did because her name means "pride." Rahab, though her back was against a wall, came to believe in a God who could make a way—a God who wouldn't judge or condemn her for trying to survive in an unjust system. God was on her side. Because God is always on the side of the oppressed.

---

5       The Polaris Project, "Sex Trafficking and LGBTQ Youth," https://polarisproject.org/sites/default/files/LGBTQ-Sex-Trafficking.pdf, (accessed November 25, 2019)."

## God Partners with Us

While God doesn't cause human oppression, God does partner with us through our oppression which sometimes, will lead to a way out of it. Partnering with God didn't come after Rahab was no longer prostituted. It didn't come after she was no longer oppressed. Partnering with God came while she was still living inside the city wall. Too many of us think we've got to be perfect before God can partner with us; we think we have to have an ordered and issue free life. But, I'm so glad that's not true. I'm so glad God is willing to partner with me even with my depression. God partners with me even with my daddy issues. I'm so glad God is willing to partner with each of us flaws and all. *B*

# *Chapter Two*

## Judges 16:4–22

*S*ometime after this, in the Sorek Valley, Samson fell in love with a woman whose name was Delilah.

**5** The rulers of the Philistines confronted her and said to her, "Seduce him and find out what gives him such great strength and what we can do to overpower him, so that we can tie him up and make him weak. Then we'll each pay you eleven hundred pieces of silver."

**6** So Delilah said to Samson, "Please tell me what gives you such great strength and how you can be tied up and made weak." **7** Samson replied to her, "If someone ties me up with seven fresh bowstrings that aren't dried out, I'll become weak. I'll be like any other person." **8** So the rulers of the Philistines brought her seven fresh bowstrings that weren't dried out, and she tied him up with them.

**9** While an ambush was waiting for her signal in an inner room, she called out to him, "Samson, the Philistines are on you!" And he snapped the bowstrings like a thread of fiber snaps when it touches a flame. So, the secret of his strength remained unknown.

**10** Then Delilah said to Samson, "You made a fool out of me and lied to me. Now please tell me how you can really be tied up!" **11** He replied to her, "If someone ties me up with new ropes that haven't been used for work, I'll become weak. I'll be like any other person."

**12** So Delilah took new ropes and tied him up with them. Then she called out to him, "Samson, the Philistines are on you!" Once again, an ambush was waiting in an inner room. Yet he snapped them from his arms like thread.

**13** And Delilah said to Samson, "Up to now, you've made a fool out of me and lied to me. Tell me how you can be tied up!" He responded to her, "If you weave the seven braids of my hair into the fabric on a loom and pull it tight with a pin, then I'll become weak. I'll be like any other person." **14** So she got him to fall asleep, wove the seven braids of his hair into the fabric on a loom, and pulled it tight with a pin.

Then she called out to him, "Samson, the Philistines are on you!" He woke up from his sleep and pulled loose the pin, the loom, and the fabric.

**15** Delilah said to him, "How can you say, 'I love you,' when you won't trust me? Three times now you've made a fool out of me and not told me what gives you such great strength!" **16** She nagged him with her words day after day and begged him until he became worn out to the point of death. **17** So he told her his whole secret. He said to her, "No razor has ever touched my head, because I've been a Nazarite for God from the time I was born. If my head is shaved, my strength will leave me, and I'll become weak. I'll be like every other person."

**18** When Delilah realized that he had told her his whole secret, she sent word to the rulers of the Philistines, "Come one more time, for he has told me his whole secret." The rulers of the Philistines came up to her and brought the silver with them.

**19** She got him to fall asleep with his head on her lap. Then she called a man and had him shave off the seven braids of Samson's hair. He began to weaken, and his strength left him. **20** She called out, "Samson, the Philistines are on you!" He woke up from his sleep and thought,

I'll escape just like the other times and shake myself free. But he didn't realize that the Lord had left him. **21** So the Philistines captured him, put out his eyes, and took him down to Gaza. They bound him with bronze chains, and he worked the grinding mill in the prison. **22** But the hair on his head began to grow again right after it had been shaved.

## What You May Not Know

⌐ Prior to his birth Samson's parents received a prophecy from a messenger of God that he was to be a Nazarite.

⌐ According to Numbers chapter 6 there were three restrictions imposed upon a Nazarite:
1) He may not drink wine, or anything made from grapes;
2) He may not cut the hair of his head;
3) He may not touch the dead, not even the body of his father or mother.

⌐ Samson was responsible for setting fire to vineyards and olive groves of certain Philistines. Then for revenge against Samson, those Philistines burned alive his wife and her father.

⌐ Read Judges 15 for the whole backstory.

## Questions for Theological Reflection

1. What have you heard about Samson?

2. What have you heard about Delilah?

3. How does what you heard about Delilah square with what you read in the text?

4. Describe Delilah's social and economic context.

5. When did Delilah lie to Samson?

6. What was Samson driven by?

7. How can our emotions adversely impact our mission and ministry?

8. What can 21st Century women learn from Delilah?

# Delilah: You Don't Own Me

**Introduction**

"You Don't Own Me" is a woman's song of resistance to gender stereotypes. It's the song of a woman staking claim to herself as an embodied human being who refuses to be trivialized or trifled with. She sings of taking herself back from any person or ideology that attempts to diminish her right to choose how she wants to live and who she wants to love. She will not be placed in a box of male expectation or fantasy. She does not need male companionship to make her whole, complete, or to feel worthy. Through her lyrics she rejects any kind of treatment deemed harmful to her sense of wholeness. So, she sings loud and self-assured, You, Don't Own, Me!

Like many women raised in a Christian church I was taught certain things about my body. Much of what I learned had the word don't in front of it:

> Don't wear your dresses too short.
> Don't wear your pants too tight.
> Don't sit with your legs too far apart.
> Don't show your cleavage.
> And, don't wear too much lipstick, especially not red lipstick.

As I studied the Bible in search of the "right ways" to handle my body, particularly as I began to think about marriage, there was one biblical passage that caused me a great deal of consternation and confusion, 1 Corinthians chapter 7. In this pericope Paul writes these words, "the wife does not have authority over her own body, but the husband does." The message this scripture communicated to me was that as women, "our body's our not really ours." Now you have to understand, as a survivor of childhood sexual abuse, the idea of not having power over my own body, the notion of it belonging to someone else, particularly a man, was problematic.

You see, one of the consequences of childhood sexual trauma, is to not feel in control of one's own body. What I mean is this, if in a person's first sexual experience they were unable to give consent, if their bodies were imposed upon, it is likely they will grow up with a belief that when certain persons want their body, they cannot say no. In other words, they don't have bodyright—the authority to decide what happens to one's own body. Others, typically people viewed as more powerful, are the ones who have rights to the bodies of survivors of sexual abuse. It's learned powerlessness. So, even though a survivor may want to say no, they feel powerless to do so. Their bodies can be screaming "no I don't want this," but nothing comes out of their mouths. Because early on, when their bodies were imposed upon, they were silenced, rendered powerless, and unable to give consent.

So, although I found the scripture problematic, in an effort to be a "good" Christian woman and wife, I submitted to what I had been taught. I functioned as if I did not have authority over my own body. My husband did. It mattered not if he was verbally and physically abusive to me. If and when he wanted my body, it was my responsibility, no matter how I felt emotionally, to make it available to him. And each time I did that, each time I handed my body over to him following an abusive verbal assault or violent tantrum, I died a little inside. Which brings me to the story of Delilah. Notice I said the story of Delilah and not Samson and Delilah. You see, Delilah is a story all by herself. And her story needs to be centered; her story is newsworthy. Her story is about more than a woman who used her feminine wiles to bring down the man of God. It's the story of a woman not the least bit interested in dying on the inside. Delilah's story is one of survival; a woman trying to live.

Now, please understand, my goal isn't to sanitize Delilah's survival strategy, but to acknowledge it as such. Delilah was trying to survive. However, the Christian church has typically read Delilah's story as if she had options. Perhaps because she took a payoff. But, just because a sista got paid, doesn't mean she had the right to refuse the Five Lords of the Philistine Pentapolis. Demonizing Delilah only diverts our attention away from the prevalence and power of the patriarchal culture in which she lived. Delilah played the hand she was dealt. Womanist Hebrew Bible Scholar Dr. Wil Gafney, in "A Womanist Midrash of Delilah: Don't Hate the Playa, Hate the Game" describes Delilah as, "a true playa for real."[6] Delilah was a badass biblical woman for sure.

But what we, the Christian church, did to Delilah—misrepresenting her—isn't unusual. You see, we have a tendency to demonize the oppressed—those who are not at the decision-making table due to their marginalized status. And, we blame them for their victimization and the strategies they use to survive.

This week I watched a video of a speech given by Oprah Winfrey at the Women's E3 Summit at the National Museum of African American History and Culture. In her speech Oprah said, "when I walk in a room and see I'm the only Black woman at the table, I wonder, "where my sista's at? It makes me wonder, who has constructed obstacles aimed at keeping them out? Because without artificial barriers we (Black women) would be represented in every room where the criteria are excellence, and discipline, and determination, and vision." When Oprah sees no Black women at the table, she acknowledges their absence. She realizes there's something more going on here. There are obstacles/barriers constructed to prevent their presence.

We haven't seen Delilah. Nor have we taken into account the context in which she lived. We missed the patriarchy in Delilah's story. Because we've demonized Delilah, we've failed to see and acknowledge the patriarchal system in which she lived. A system which forced her into a situation she couldn't refuse.

So, here's takeaway #1 from Delilah's story:
If we're serious and want to dismantle patriarchy or any social injustice, we must first see it. Once we see it we must acknowledge its adverse impact on

---

6        Wil Gafney, "A Womanist Midrash of Delilah: Don't Hate the Playa Hate the Game," in *Womanist Interpretations of the Bible: Expanding the Discourse*, eds. Gay L. Byron and Vanessa Lovelace (Atlanta, SBL Press, 2016), 49.

human beings—whomever they may be.

**Independent and Dangerous**

The book of Judges describes Delilah as an independent, free thinking, single woman, with her own crib and financial resources. There's no mention of any parents, husband, siblings, girlfriends, extended family, and we don't know her occupation or how she made money to maintain her independence. She appears in Judges as a woman alone—a precarious place for a woman. With no male to protect her she was a woman vulnerable. Yet, somehow, she managed.

Some of us know a little something about making it without a spouse or partner. Some of us know a little something about piecing together an income. We work a little over here, and a little over there to make rent, pay the utilities, and car the note. Delilah was an independent woman who pieced together a living for herself in a society of patriarchy, where male desire, ideology, and perspectives were centered and normative. In patriarchal societies, the lives of women, children, servants and warriors are owned by the patriarchs, whose interests they served.

Patriarchy desperately tries to control women's bodies. At one time, women in China were forced to bind their feet to make them appear smaller, which was more attractive to men. Even today some women, in order to please the pallets of men, carry on the practice. Similarly, if you're a girl between the ages of 8–12 living in Cameroon, you may have to suffer through breast ironing, a painful procedure where mothers take a stone and repeatedly press in on the chest of their daughters to flatten their breast. Mother's subject their daughters to this procedure in an attempt to protect them from looking too mature which places them at risk of rape. In the United States, in some conservative evangelical circle's daughters pledge their virginity to their fathers and make purity pacts, promising not to have sex until marriage.

But Delilah was an independent woman with no father or husband to control what she did with her body,

> where she took it,
>
> what she thought,
>
> how she reasoned, or
>
> how she made decisions.

Because she was able to provide for herself, Delilah was able to survive to some degree, outside the patriarchy.

But maybe just maybe Delilah wanted more than survival.

With the money she would receive from the Five Lords, which in today's economy may have exceeded a million dollars—some scholars suggest it could have been as much as a billion dollar—Delilah would've been able to not just survive, she could thrive. A small price to pay for handing over a man she barely knew, didn't love, and who had been bad news already to two other women and their communities.

Wil Gafney characterizes Delilah as a self-possessed, self-maintained woman who is bad news to patriarchy. In her text Gafney says, "an independent woman with her own resources like Delilah, is dangerous to patriarchy."[7] Furthermore, when a woman has bodyright, like Delilah, she is presumed dangerous and needs to be controlled. After all, it was believed that a woman's body and her sensuality could be used to bring down the strongest of men. Early Church Father's like, Tertullian and Augustine taught the Church the dangers of women and our bodies, characterizing us as "the devils gateway"[8] and "temptress."[9] A woman's body therefore had to be controlled.

So, here's takeaway #2 from Delilah's story:
If patriarchy is to be dismantled, we must help those who seek to do so find ways to survive and thrive independent of the system. The question then becomes, how can we create opportunities for women's independence—

---

7    Ibid, 65.
8    Earl Lavender, "Tertullian – Against Women?" in *On the Apparel of Women*, 1.1.1–2, quoted in Osburn, *Essays on Women in Earliest Christianity, Vol. 2*, 332–333
9    Augustine, *Literal Commentary on Genesis*, IX.5, quoted in Tucker and Liefeld, *Daughters of the Church*, 123.

how can we help marginalized groups have their own.

## Males and Bodyright

There was a second part of that 1 Corinthians text that I found interesting. Although Paul said, "the husband does not have authority over his own body, but the wife does," men rarely seem inconvenienced or encumbered by such stipulations. Men seem to have full control over their bodies. From what I could tell, men even had the power and privilege to impose their bodies on women. Men seem to have societal approval to use their bodies as instruments of violence when threatened; cloth their bodies in whatever they chose without garnering criticism from church folk; and appear shirtless in public, whether it's running up and down a basketball court, mowing the lawn, or just walking down the street on a smoldering hot summer day. Males, no matter their age, appear, at least to me, to have bodyright. But not women and girls. But this isn't news to any of us is it? Most of us have been socialized to adapt to this gender-dualism in which males are superior to females. I think one of the reasons we adapt is because we see gender-dualism in the biblical text.

## Gender-Dualism

Nowhere are gender-dualisms more glaring than in the book of Judges. Several chapters detail Samson's sexual exploits and murderous tirades. Yet, Delilah is characterized as a whore. Samson on the other hand is pitied as merely foolish.

But if we look closely, we can see Delilah as a woman who resisted gender-dualisms. In no way is she inferior to the man in her life. In fact, she beat him at his own game. She resisted normative categories of women's roles and gender stereotypes. Which is why I'm fascinated by the biblical story of Delilah. When I think of present-day Delilah's, women who resist gender-dualisms, I think of Rhianna, Alicia Keys, Pink, Angela Bassett, Oprah, Queen Latifa, India Arie, Gabrielle Sidibe, and Laverne Cox.

Present Day Delilah's are taking back their bodies from patriarchal imaginations. Present Day Delilah's will not be boxed in by gender-dualisms. Present day Delilah's tell their own stories. Write their own narratives. Present day Delilah's resist ownership.

So, here's takeaway #3 from Delilah's story:

If we're serious and want to dismantle patriarchy, we must tell our own stories. We must tell how we've been adversely impacted by it, what it has cost us, our families, our communities, and how we survived and thrived in the midst of it. We must tell our stories of resistance. We have to say more than "by God's grace" or "God got me through." How did God get you through? That's the question people need answered. Well, Delilah was given an offer she couldn't refuse. That's how she thrived. Sadly, surviving and thriving in the midst of patriarchy meant hurting another person. It was Samson or her. Sometimes, it's going to be the other person who suffers. Other times it just might be you. Patriarchy isn't pretty and dismantling it isn't going to be pretty. People are going to get hurt. Just ask Jesus. Jesus resisted every power and principality designed to own the human mind, body, and spirit. Yet, he resisted. Jesus told the powers, "You Don't Own Me." *B*

# *Chapter Three*

## 1 Chronicles 7:20–24

The sons of Ephraim: Shuthelah, and Bered his son, Tahath his son, Eleadah his son, Tahath his son, **21** Zabad his son, Shuthelah his son, and Ezer and Elead. Now the people of Gath, who were born in the land, killed them, because they came down to raid their cattle. **22** And their father Ephraim mourned many days, and his brothers came to comfort him. **23** Ephraim went into his wife, and she conceived and bore a son; and he named him Beriah, because disaster had befallen his house. **24** His daughter was Sheerah, who built both Lower and Upper Beth-horon, and Uzzen-sheerah.

# What You May Not Know

- Sheerah means remnant.

- In the Greek language, the book of Chronicles is titled Paraleipomena and means "things left behind" or "left-over."[10]

- Sheerah is mentioned only once and in only one verse of the Hebrew Bible.

- Sheerah is the only female designated and identified as a builder of cities in the entire Bible.

- Some scholars are "suspicious" of the inclusion of Sheerah in 1 Chronicles 7:24, calling her presence "intrusive" as it "interrupts" the linear genealogy of Ephraim in verses 20–21, 25 and 27.[11]

- Sheerah's identity is ambiguous. It's uncertain whether she's the daughter of Ephraim or his son Beriah.

- Ephraim is the grandson of Jacob and the son of Joseph. In Genesis 48, Jacob on his death bed, gave Ephraim the blessing to share in his inheritance. Although he was younger than his brother Manasseh, Ephraim was given the blessing of the first born by Jacob. Jacob believed Ephraim's descendants would be greater than his brothers.

- Beriah means misfortune, unlucky, and disaster. It could also mean "gift."[12]

10    Funlola Olojede in her 2011 Dissertation, "Unsung Heroins of the the Hebrew Bible: A Contextual Theological Reading from the Perspective of Woman Wisdom" interprets the LXX title, Paraleopomena as "things omitted from" or "left out" of the books of Samuel–Kings (Braun 1986:xix; Japhet 1993:1; Selman 1994:19; Tuell 2001:1; Kniooppoers 2004:49; Dirksen 2005:2 and Klein 2006:1).
11    Ibid, 138.

– Linear Genealogies only contain names of persons who are socially significant to the author's contemporary concerns.[13]

# Questions for Theological Reflection

1. Why might the Chronicler have included Sheerah and her accomplishments in the pericope?

2. Compare and contrast how the narrative describes the roles of Sheerah and her mother.

3. Discuss the contemporary significance of these different roles for women.

4. Why is Sheerah's story important for preaching and biblical teaching?

5. What happens when the stories of the marginalized are skipped over? How are women and girls adversely impacted. How is the church adversely impacted?

6. What impact did the criminal activity of Ezer and Elead have on the family?

7. Discuss a time when a family member's decision adversely impacted you?

8. Has there been a time when the negative behavior or decision of a church member impacted your life or the life of the church you attended? If so, how was it handled?

9. How did Ephraim handle his grief? Name a few ways you handle your grief? How can communities of color handle collective grief?

12      Ibid, 140.
13      Robert R Wilson. "Genealogy and History" in the *Biblical World*, New Haven: Yale University Press, 35.

10. Ephraim named Beriah misfortune. How important is naming? Identity the names of people who are important or who have shaped your identity.

11. How might the Holy Spirit be using Sheerah's story in your life?

# Sheerah: Are You Built to Last?

## Introduction

Leaving a legacy has been a central thought in my mind. What will I leave behind after I've gone to be with the ancestors? I just heard someone say, "it's not what you leave for people, it's what you leave in them." How would my being in the world have impacted it positively? Who will be better because they had something to do with me?

## Sheerah Was Skipped Over

Until recently I had never read about, nor heard of, sista Sheerah. I knew about her father Ephraim, and her uncle Manasseh. They were sons of Joseph and his African wife, Aesnath. But not Sheerah.

Sheerah was hidden in Ephraim's genealogy. Like some of you, I don't like reading genealogies; too many names that I cannot pronounce. So, like you, I skip over genealogies.

## We're Skipped Over

When have you been skipped over? Have ever been treated like you were insignificant, like you don't count, like your story doesn't matter?

You ever been dissed: discounted, disrespected, or disregarded, rendered invisible. Have you ever been ignored? Sheerah will not be ignored. We will not skip over her today.

Sheerah is no longer invisible. Because she has something to tell us; something that just might transform our thinking.

Sheerah's life can teach us something about the value, worth, and the ingenuity of women.

So, who is this woman called Sheerah?

## The Sister of Misfortune

It's difficult to determine if Sheerah's father was Ephraim or Beriah. If

Beriah was her father, Sheerah is the daughter of Misfortune. If Ephraim was her Father, then Sheerah is the sister of misfortune. Let me explain.

Ephraim had several sons, two of them, Ezer and Elead were criminals. They were killed by the people of Gath for stealing their cattle. Upon learning of their death, Ephraim was distraught. So, what did he do? He made love to his wife. She became pregnant and gave birth to a son. While apparently still grieving Ephraim named his baby boy Beriah, which means misfortune. The Message Bible interprets the Hebrew word Beriah as, unlucky. The way the text reads, scholars aren't clear if Sheerah was the daughter of Beriah or the daughter of Ephraim. Either way, misfortune is a terrible legacy to live into.

## People of Misfortune

Perhaps you can relate. Maybe you've lived through one disaster after another; you've seen enough trouble to last a lifetime; when you look over your shoulder you see hardship, adversity, trials and tribulations. Misfortune. Little has gone your way in life. Most of the time you feel like you have an X on your forehead as a target for mistreatment. Misfortune.

But I'm here to tell you that no matter what you were born into, no matter what your past has been, no matter where you've come from, no matter what misfortune befalls you, you don't have to let your past hold your future hostage. God can bring you out; God is able to deliver. God is able to set your feet on a solid rock. Don't you know that God is notorious for making a way out of no way! Sister Sheerah stands as a witness.

Although she was a sister of misfortune, she was also an accomplished daughter. Hear her testimony, "His daughter was Sheerah, she built (can somebody say, she built) both Lower and Upper Beth-horon, and Uzzen-sheerah."

Sheerah was a city builder. Not of one city, not two cities, but Sheerah built three cities.

Not her brother's, but Sheerah. Not her daddy, but Sheerah. In fact, her brothers, Ezer and Elead had been disappointments to their father. But not Sheerah. She was accomplished and productive. But, how could this be? She was a woman. She was a woman living in a patriarchal, androcentric culture. A culture where women could not own property. In fact, women were property! But not Sheerah, she was a builder. Now that's quite an accomplishment. Why? Because in Ancient Israel the role of building was assigned to males only. Sheerah is the only woman recorded in the Old Testament to build cities. Building cities was a sign of God's blessings and favor.

In 2 Chronicles 26 the Bible says that "as long as [King Uzziah] sought the Lord, God made him prosper…he rebuilt cities in the territory of Ashdod and elsewhere among the Philistines. King Uzziah was a city builder. The text makes it clear that as long as King Uzziah pursued God, that God gave him success. Sheerah must have had a deep abiding commitment to follow the ways of God. So, she has something to teach us. Let's see what this woman of faith has to teach us about building. What did she have on the inside that enabled her to succeed on the outside? I believe Sheerah had what one author calls "It!"

**Sheerah Had "It!"**
In a book titled *It: How Churches and Leaders Can Get It and Keep It*, Mark Groeschel identifies characteristics of successful churches and leaders. He says these churches and leaders have It! He says, "Some ministries have it. Some don't. Most churches want it. Few have it. When a church has it, everyone can tell. And when one doesn't…everyone can tell." He says the same is true with leaders. Some leaders have it. Some don't. "You either have it, or you don't because, it is real, it is genuine, it is not the result of external factors, and there is no faking it."[14]

Mark says, you can walk into a congregation and know immediate-

---

14    Mark Groeschel, *It: How Churches and Leaders Can Get It and Keep It* (Grand Rapids: Zondervan, 2008), Preface, Kindle.

ly if IT is present, it is unmistakable! It is always unique. It is always powerful. It is always life changing. He also says that it has a downside. It attracts
critics. It is controversial. Many people don't understand it. It is hard to
find, but it's impossible to miss. Sheerah, my sisters and brothers had it!

Because Sheerah had It!, she was a builder.


**She was Daring**

There's another reason I believe Sheerah was able to build. She possessed
a daring spirit. To be daring is to be bold, audacious, adventurous, uncon-
ventional, and courageous. Sheerah dared to dream.

Sheerah didn't just wake up one morning and say, "Hmmm, I think
I will build three cities today." No, she dreamed it. Perhaps like her great
grandfather Joseph the dreamer, she too learned to believe that God could
speak to her through her dreams. Perhaps she learned that she could trust
the God who gave her those dreams. Like her great grandfather, she did not
allow others to be dream-snatchers. Joseph's brothers were dream-snatchers, at least they tried to be. The Bible says, "Joseph had a dream, and when
he told it to his brothers, they hated him all the more." But Joseph trusted
God with his life and with his dreams; yes, he was thrown in a pit; yes, he
was put in jail; yes, he was falsely accused and thrown in jail again. Daring to dream will cost you! And yet, God rescued Joseph and enabled him
to save the lives of all who lived in Egypt. Sheerah, like Joseph, dared to
dream.

But Sheerah didn't just dream; she went after it. Sheerah imple-
mented her dream, and thus, pursued her destiny.

Pursuing our destiny means willing to go through the preparation
process! No shortcuts or easy way out. Sheerah had to learn how to build
cities. She had to learn how to manage people and get along with them.
Pursuing her destiny meant long hours, sleepless nights, and overcoming
obstacles. It meant resolving conflicts and supervising men who didn't think
she had a right to do what God called her to do! Ouch! It means not being

afraid to be the only one. Having the courage to be a trailblazer. It's counting the cost; putting in work, and trusting that your labor will not be in vain in the Lord. You see, when you are built to last, what you build will last.

## Sheerah was Built to Last

Sheerah built three cities, Upper and Lower Beth-horon, and Uzzen-sheerah. The third city, Uzzen-Sheerah means, listen to Sheerah. Listen to Sheerah, listen to someone who did it. Listen to a woman. Listen to a woman who has survived the fire. Listen to a woman who knows what it means to be on the margins, silenced and skipped over. Listen to a woman who overcame the odds, who trusted God enough to risk. Listen to the woman whose works speak for her. Let me tell you about the cities that Sheerah built and why she is built to last.

In the book of Joshua chapter 10 the Bible tells the story of a battle, one that resulted in God causing the sun to stand still. Starting in Joshua 10:6 the text says,

"the Gibeonites…sent word to Joshua in the camp at Gilgal.,'Do not abandon your servants. Come up to us quickly and save us! Help us, because all the Amorite kings from the hill country have joined forces against us.' So, Joshua marched from Gilgal with his entire army, including all the best fighting men. The Lord said to Joshua, 'Do not be afraid of them; I have given them into your hand. Not one of them will be able to withstand you…' Joshua took them by surprise. The Lord threw them into confusion before Israel, who defeated them in a great victory at Gibeon. Israel pursued them along the road going up to Beth-Horon and cut them down…As they fled before Israel on the road down from Beth-Horon… the Lord hurled hailstones down on them from the sky, and more died from the hailstones than were killed by the swords of the Israelites. On the day the Lord gave the Amorites over to Israel, Joshua said to the Lord in the presence of Israel: 'O, sun, stand still…so the sun stood still and the moon stopped.'"

Beloved, the cities that Sheerah built hundreds of years earlier were the site of one of Israel's greatest victories. The pass between Upper Beth-Horon and Lower Beth-Horon provided the space needed for Joshua to drive the Amorites into utter defeat.

Remember I told you that when you're built to last, what you build lasts. Well, those cities that Sheerah built are still standing in Palestine.

Sheerah was built to last: her name, her reputation, her strength, her courage, her dream, her determination, her destiny, and the cities she built. Thank God we have Sheerah as our example.

So, the question for us is this:

Are we building our lives in such a way that what we build will last?

Are you built to last? Because it Is possible to build a life that lasts. You see, Sheerah is not the only person in the Bible who was built to last.

## Jesus Christ is Built to Last

I know a man, like no other man, Jesus the Christ is built to last. He was born in a manger, but he was built to last. He was rejected by those closest to him, but he is built to last. He was betrayed by one of his own, but he is built to last; he was hung on a cross, crucified between two thieves, buried in another man's tomb, remained there three days, but do not fret, he is built to last. One Sunday morning the grave couldn't hold him, and the rock couldn't hide him, the power of God raised him from the dead, Christ is Built to Last! When we build our lives on the life and teachings of Jesus Christ, what we build will last. *B*

# Chapter Four

## Numbers 26: 1–4; 52–54; 27:1–11

After the plague the LORD said to Moses and to Eleazar son of Aaron the priest, **2** "Take a census of the whole congregation of the Israelites, from twenty years old and upward, by their ancestral houses, everyone in Israel able to go to war." **3** Moses and Eleazar the priest spoke with them in the plains of Moab by the Jordan opposite Jericho, saying, **4** "Take a census of the people, from twenty years old and upward," as the LORD commanded Moses…

**52** The LORD spoke to Moses, saying: 53 To these the land shall be apportioned for inheritance according to the number of names. 54 To a large tribe you shall give a large inheritance, and to a small tribe you shall give a small inheritance; every tribe shall be given its inheritance according to its enrollment.

**27:1** Then the daughters of Zelophehad came forward. Zelophehad was son of Hepher son of Gilead son of Machir son of Manasseh son of Joseph, a member of the Manassite clans. The names of his daughters were: Mahlah, Noah, Hoglah, Milcah, and Tirzah. **2** They stood before Moses, Eleazar the priest, the leaders, and all the congregation, at the entrance of the tent of meeting, and they said, **3** "Our father died in the wilderness; he was not among the company of those who gathered themselves together against the LORD in the company of Korah, but died for his own sin; and he had no sons.

**4** Why should the name of our father be taken away from his clan because he had no son? Give to us a possession among our father's brothers."

**5** Moses brought their case before the LORD. **6** And the LORD spoke to Moses, saying: **7** The daughters of Zelophehad are right in what they are saying; you shall indeed let them possess an inheritance among their father's brothers and pass the inheritance of their father on to them. **8** You shall also say to the Israelites, "If a man dies, and has no son, then you shall pass his inheritance on to his daughter. **9** If he has no daughter, then you shall give his inheritance to his brothers. **10** If he has no brothers, then you shall give his inheritance to his father's brothers. **11** And if his father has no brothers, then you shall give his inheritance to the nearest kinsman of his clan, and he shall possess it. It shall be for the Israelites a statute and ordinance, as the LORD commanded Moses."

## What You May Not Know

⌐ Following the deaths of the remaining Israelites of the Wilderness generation, a new military census was taken prior to the occupation of the promised land.

⌐ Sons were sole heirs of father's property/land upon his death.

⌐ Sons were the offspring of father's sexual union with:

| | |
|---|---|
| Wives | Concubines |
| Maids | Slaves and/or Harlots |

# Questions for Theological Reflection

- In verses 52–54 of chapter 26 does it describe equality or equity? What are differences between equality and equity.

- When did the daughters of Zelophehad come forward and why might they have come when they did?

- How many sisters came forward? What impact may that number have had on the conversation?

- What are and/or have been some unjust laws in America?

- Discuss one of two unjust laws and how they were made just.

- What unjust laws does are you passionate to make right?

- What can we learn from this narrative to help us in our fight for justice?

# Sisters with the Audacity to Dream Big

Martin Luther King Jr., and Moses are two distinct stories of two spiritual leaders called to liberate oppressed people. And I can say with certainty of both men, that "if it hadn't been for the women", neither could have accomplished their God ordained mission.

With the signing of the Civil Rights Act of 1964, the work of liberation for Black folk didn't end. Even today, Black women are still a marginalized group. James Cone describes society's view of Black women as, "the underside of the underside." Black women are yet in need of liberation.

In the passage in Numbers we discover a similar scenario, Moses' work of liberation didn't end with setting Israelites free from Egyptian bondage. There were women in their number, women with a dream of freedom of their own. Freedom to be self-sufficient, as self-sufficient as possible in a patriarchal society in Ancient Israel. Women who dreamed of land ownership, which meant controlling their own destiny as much as possible.

There were in fact, five women, sisters whose father died on the trek from the stew pots of Egypt to the promised land of Canaan. Their father's death was untimely and inconvenient. You see, Zelophehad, the father of these five sisters, had no sons. And, according to Jewish law and custom, daughters had no right to land ownership. An inconvenient injustice for sisters on the verge of crossing the Jordan into the land flowing with milk and honey, the land of Canaan. God promised them that in Canaan every Israelite family would have a portion of land to call their own. Land that was fruitful and fertile. Land that would yield crops and provide financial profit ensuring economic stability for generations to come. But not for these five sisters, or any other Israelite women left without father or brothers. These five women were up against the injustice of patriarchy. But, they had big dreams. Dreams just like those of Ella Baker.

## Ella Baker Dreams

Characterized by many as the Mother of the Civil Rights Movement, Ella Jo Baker, had the audacity to dream big. Her dream was for Black people to create our own solutions for the myriad injustices that plague us and our communities. She had the audacity to dream a big dream that black people could join together and peaceably insist that they were deserving of basic human rights. And, Ella's dreams had feet.

Born in Norfolk, Virginia, Ella Baker grew up in rural North Carolina, where she developed a deep sense of self-respect. Her parents shared their food with hungry neighbors; her grandmother told how she endured a savage whipping rather than agree to marry a man chosen for her by a master. Her grandmother's pride and resilience in the face of racism and injustice continued to inspire Ms. Baker throughout her life.

As a granddaughter of slaves, Ella, graduated valedictorian in 1927 from Shaw University in Raleigh, North Carolina. Even as a student, Ella challenged school policies that she thought were unfair. After graduating, she moved to New York City and began joining social activist organizations. She spent nearly half a century raising the political consciousness of Americans, and played a major role in three of the 20th century's most influential civil rights groups: The NAACP, the Southern Christian Leadership Conference (SCLC) and Student Nonviolent Coordinating Committee (SNCC).

Utilizing her iron will and a gift for listening, Baker helped local leaders carefully craft and implement targeted campaigns against lynching, for job training and for black teachers to get equal pay. Baker was passionate about and adept at recognizing latent leadership in those she considered emerging young activists. She was a mentor and trainer who possessed the finely tuned skill of developing future social activist leaders. Among the participants at one of her workshops was an NAACP member from Montgomery, Alabama, named Rosa Parks. Even today in the 21st Century, the Children's Defense Fund has The Ella Baker Training Institute in association with their Freedom Schools. On the Children's Defense Fund website, it says the following: "Each year, exceptional servant leader interns are selected as Ella Baker trainers (EBT) to lead the Ella Baker Child Policy Training Institutes".

The website explains their rationale for naming the Training Institute after Ella:

"Ella Baker was an integral leader in the Civil Rights Movement, organizing and mentoring hundreds of young people, Marian Wright Edelman among them. Often a powerful behind-the-scenes advisor to close colleagues like Dr. Martin Luther King, Jr., Ella Baker believed in shared leadership and encouraged young people to find and lift their own voices. She understood the need for hard, daily, persistent work, and was an institution builder."

Ella Baker had the audacity to dream Big; and her dreams had long term implications. Ella Baker died on her 83rd birthday, on December 13, 1986, in New York City, but her life and accomplishments were chronicled in the 1981 documentary Fundi: The Story of Ella Baker. "Fundi" was her nickname, which comes from a Swahili word that means a person who passes down a craft to the next generation.

To dream big means our dreams are not just for us. Our big dreams do not end in our generation but are realized for generations to come.

## Five Sisters Dream Big

That's why I love the story of the daughters of Zelophehad. They looked adversity in the eye and decided they would not be defined by their circumstances but collectively, they would be agents for change. They had the audacity to dream big.

Five sisters, whom many have never heard about. Their story is in the Bible, but receive little press or fanfare, just like the women in the civil rights movement, Mah'lah, Noah, Hog'lah, Mil'cah, and Tir'zah, had to contend with the injustice of sexism, patriarchy, and economic insecurity. Even so, they had the audacity to dream big. They too had iron will and the strength to do something gutsy, something courageous. They did something no other women had done before them, they showed up.

## They Showed Up

They showed up to the tent of meeting. The place where the big boys hung out—Moses, Eleazar the High Priest, and the other male leaders of the Israelite community.

Listen, if we're going to dream big we've got to show up. We've got to be present and accounted for. We've got to push past our fears and do the hard work of showing up, even in our own lives. We cannot sit idly by and wait for someone to give us something they think we ought to have. We've got to show up. When we show up, we're communicating something about what we believe about others and ourselves. There are no throwaways. Mah'lah, Noah, Hog'lah, Mil'cah, and Tir'zah would not allow their community to marginalize them, they refused to be thrown away. They had the audacity to dream and so, they showed up at the tent to meeting.

But not only did these sista's show up, they stood up.

## They Stood Up

Standing up has to do with three things, courage, conviction, and commitment. The daughters of Zelophehad had courage to do something different. They were not intimidated by male power. They had a conviction that what they were doing was right and just. And they had a commitment that despite the odds, they would not give up or back down.

Finally, these sista's also spoke up.

## They Spoke Up

They were advocates that spoke up at just the right time. They spoke up when Moses was in the tent of meeting talking about marriage and inheritance laws. These women knew something about the Law of God. And so, they presented their case at just the right time and to the right person. They didn't spend their time complaining and belly aching about how the system wasn't treating them fair. Instead, they challenged the system.

The interesting thing here is that they took on the system not strictly for themselves, but for others. They were concerned about their father's lineage. They spoke up because they were concerned about those that were coming after them, their children and their children's children.

So, what became of their dream? We find that answer in Numbers 36 verse 5, the text reads like this, "Then Moses commanded the Israelites according to the word of the Lord…" Moses did what the Lord told him to do. The law was changed.

The Daughters of Zelophehad and other women in the Israelite community would now be able to inherit land from their fathers. What's most remarkable about this turn of events is that the new law didn't just impact the Israelite community or these 5 sisters. This change in the law had long range ramifications, down to you and I. Their dream blesses women even today.

Beloved, do you have a dream? I hope so. I hope you dream of eradicating every principality, every power, every ounce of spiritual wickedness that marginalizes and oppresses God's human creation. I hope you have the audacity to dream big. *B*

# Chapter Five

## Exodus 1:15–2:10 (CEB)

*T*he king of Egypt spoke to two Hebrew midwives named Shiphrah and Puah: **16** "When you are helping the Hebrew women give birth and you see the baby being born, if it's a boy, kill him. But if it's a girl, you can let her live." **17** Now the two midwives respected God so they didn't obey the Egyptian king's order. Instead, they let the baby boys live.

**18** So the king of Egypt called the two midwives and said to them, "Why are you doing this? Why are you letting the baby boys live?"

**19** The two midwives said to Pharaoh, "Because Hebrew women aren't like Egyptian women. They're much stronger and give birth before any midwives can get to them." **20** So God treated the midwives well, and the people kept on multiplying and became very strong. **21** And because the midwives respected God, God gave them households of their own.

**22** Then Pharaoh gave an order to all his people: "Throw every baby boy born to the Hebrews into the Nile River, but you can let all the girls live."

**2:1** Now a man from Levi's household married a Levite woman.

**2** The woman became pregnant and gave birth to a son. She saw that the baby was healthy and beautiful, so she hid him for three months. **3** When she couldn't hide him any longer, she took a reed basket and sealed it up with black tar. She put the child in the basket and set the basket among the reeds at the riverbank. **4** The baby's older sister stood watch nearby to see what would happen to him.

**5** Pharaoh's daughter came down to bathe in the river, while her women servants walked along beside the river. She saw the basket among the reeds, and she sent one of her servants to bring it to her. **6** When she opened it, she saw the child. The boy was crying, and she felt sorry for him. She said, "This must be one of the Hebrews' children."

**7** Then the baby's sister said to Pharaoh's daughter, "Would you like me to go and find one of the Hebrew women to nurse the child for you?"

**8** Pharaoh's daughter agreed, "Yes, do that." So, the girl went and called the child's mother. **9** Pharaoh's daughter said to her, "Take this child and nurse it for me, and I'll pay you for your work." So, the woman took the child and nursed it. **10** After the child had grown up, she brought him back to Pharaoh's daughter, who adopted him as her son. She named him Moses, "because," she said, "I pulled him out of the water."

## What You May Not Know

**King of Egypt**
- Pharaoh
- Supreme Ruler

**Midwife**
- An office of great responsibility
- Typically had no children of their own/Barren

- Helped other women do what they could not do
- A ministry of saving lives

**Levite Woman**
- Her name was Jocabed
- She was the mother of Moses

**The Baby's Sister**
- Miriam

# Questions for Theological Reflection

1. What was the motivation undergirding the Egyptian King's desire to assassinate baby boys?

2. In the 21st Century can you identify groups of people that seemed marked for assassination? Who are they? Why do you think modern day Pharaoh's want them eliminated?

3. What are types of spiritual and emotional assassination that some people experience?

4. Name some modern day Shiphrah and Puah's—women who resist unjust laws and edicts.

5. There are at least six women identified in these two passages. Who are they?

6. How are these women connected?

7. Around what issues can women/people of different races, cultures, and

socio-economic classes connect and work to eradicate and dismantle.

8. Do you have a personal mission statement that guides your life? If so, in what ways is your personal mission life saving for people marked for assassination?

# If It Wasn't For Six Badass Women

**Introduction**

It's not safe being a cis-gendered woman and it's most certainly not safe being a woman who identifies as transgender!

In America and around the globe, women and girls are in danger! Every single day women and girls are brutally and often fatally raped, sometimes even in public. Women are in danger! Every 15 seconds a woman is beaten. It's not safe being female. Every single day at least 3 women die as a result of domestic abuse. Women are in danger.

Each day, girls as young as five years old, are forced into prostitution by a family member. It's not safe being female. Women and girls are in danger. But for the most part, the world doesn't seem to care. As a preacher and pastor, it grieves me to say that not even the church seems to care. At least, not enough to do anything radical or revolutionary about it!

Yes, there are pockets of people groups in this country and abroad who do lend their voices, donate their money, and offer their services to help vulnerable and marginalized people, including women and girls. But it's not enough! More must be done.

More people need to care. More people need to put feet on their faith and care that 1 in 4 girls and 1 in 6 boys are sexually abused by their 18th birthday; more people need to care that Domestic Human Trafficking generates $32 billion in revenue annually; more people need to care that 276 girls were abducted from their school in Nigeria and are reported as being sold by their abductors for $12! More people must care enough to act!"

**Chingona Fire**

Here's what else I think. I think we need a church who cares. We need a church with women (and men) like the women in the first 2 chapters of Exodus; women who committed acts of civil disobedience in order to save the lives of vulnerable children.

Recently I learned a new phrase from a poem in a Huffpost article, that describes such women—chingona Fire. [15] The word chingona isn't a word you're likely to hear outside of a Latinx community. In fact, it's Spanish slang term. The first word of the phrase, chingona means, "bad ass woman."[16] The second word, fire, represents the passion by which these bad ass women operate. Now, although the word "chingona" is a Spanish term, it isn't restricted to Latinas.

The poem, submitted by Angela Aguirre, a Chicana Feminist, Poet, and Activist describes a chingona as "any woman who chooses to live life on her own terms. PERIOD. A chingona is unbothered, unbought, and unbossed. She is not concerned with your opinion about her use of hood slang in collegiate settings; she's not concerned about the length of her skirt at a job interview, nor anybody's bullshit respectability politics."[17]

Ms. Aguirre's poem defines a chingona in even more detail as she explains,

"some chingona's are educated and some are self-taught. What truly defines a chingona is their ability to harness their fire. Chingona fire is a revolutionary act. An act of resistance. It is as much about lipstick as it is about fighting the patriarchy. Chingona fire is the ability to convey an entire message with your eyebrows alone. It is loving yourself, regardless, and taking no shit and refusing to apologize for your existence. It is raising your voice when others try to silence it. It is the reason you survive, not because of luck. But because the fire within you burns brighter than the one around you. Chingona fire is communal. It is believing in a power greater than yourself."

Mic drop!

We need a church full of chingona's—Badass people to be a voice for

15      Angela Aguirre, "How I Define My Chingona Fire," *Huffpost*, January 25, 2017, https://www.huffpost.com/entry/how-i-define-my-chingona-fire_b_5887de69e4b0a53ed-60c6a35
16      Ibid.
17      Ibid.

women and children in danger. We need a church who cares enough to act! We need a church willing to be Badass!"

## Six Badass Women

We need only investigate the biblical text to discover a few badass women! There are six right here in the first two chapters of Exodus. In our teaching passage we actually find six badass women. They are: Shiphrah, Puah, Jochebed, the mother of Moses, Miriam Moses' sister, Pharaoh's Daughter, and The Maid (s) of Pharaoh's Daughter. As I studied this text and the characteristics of these six women, I identified what I call the:

## 4 R's of Badass Women:

First of all, when I explored the characteristics of the first two women, Shiphrah & Puah, the R that came to mind was *resist*. Their resistance was demonstrated by their refusal to do violence of any kind. They resisted the command of Pharaoh to kill children—baby boys in particular. They refused to behave in a way that was antithetical to who they were. They were life givers. They were midwives, women with a calling to bring new life into the world. Pharaoh asked them to violate their own sense of conscious; he wanted them to deny all that God had called, crafted, and created them to be and to do. And that was to give life. And so, they resisted.

A badass woman learns to resist violence whether it is verbal, physical, or emotional. A badass woman cultivates the courage to intervene, like Shiphrah and Puah and not be intimidated by people with power. I know that can be difficult. But, these two sista's did it. I believe they were able to resist Pharaoh's edict because they had allegiance to a higher power, they referenced God. Resisting violence is to recognize that there is a power greater than the principalities and power with which we wrestle with each day.

Another R that characterizes what it means to be a badass woman is *risk*. The mother of Moses, in order to save his life had to take a risk. Following his birth, Moses mother hid her son for 3 months. Can you imagine that? Now, for those of you who've had children you know they can be a little loud at times. They cry when we don't want them to cry and at the most inopportune times. But somehow Moses' mother was able to hide him such that his crying didn't alert those who sought to kill him. She risked her own life to save his.

Taking a risk to love and protect children who may not make it out of their environment alive means taking a risk. There are children today, and some of you school teachers know that full well, the trauma some of the kids in your classes experience. You may not know the exact nature of it, but you can tell the children are not safe at home, in their communities, walking down the street, playing music, or even going to school. But you love them; you teach them; you create opportunities for them to share and talk about what troubles them. You do this because you don't know if they're going to make it out of their environment alive. And so, you take a risk.

Shiprah, Puah, and Jochebed believed in the future of Moses even though it looked bleak. Taking a risk on someone when it appears all the odds are against them is what badass women do.

In order to take the kinds of risks I'm talking about requires that we see people. I mean really see them. Get to know them. Push past our preconceived judgments and stereotypes and see people, especially people who are different from us. No one deserves to be overlooked. Which means we need to stop walking around this world with rose colored glasses acting like everything for everybody is alright just because it's alright where you live, where you hangout, and where your children go to school. It's not alright for everybody. We need to see them.

The next R that characterizes, at least for me, what it means to be a badass woman is *ready*. We've got to be ready. Growing up in my neighborhood the Old folks would often say, "if you stay ready you don't have to get ready." Ready is being prepared for action. Miriam, the sister of Moses was ready. I like that the text said she stood by and watched her brother float down the Nile River.

Miriam positioned herself in such as way as to be able to see where he was going and what he was going into. By stationing herself, Miriam was able to see down the Nile, where he was going, where he was headed.

We need badass women who can see where we're headed, where we're going. Miriam made herself aware of what was happening in the life of someone she loved and wanted to protect. She was looking for the crocodiles, she was looking for water moccasins, she was looking to ward off any danger her brother might encounter. By stationing herself she wanted to make sure he had safe passage. Badass women pay attention to what's happening to the most vulnerable people in their city.

Badass women have communal concerns. Badass women look for opportunities to advocate, to heal, to partner in creating a world where the most vulnerable are safe and able to thrive.

The final R representing what is means to be a badass woman is *recruit*. Sisters, we've got to learn how to recruit. We cannot do everything all by ourselves. Now, I know you're a strong Black woman and you've got chingona fire, but you cannot change the world by yourself. You cannot save lives alone.

To recruit is to connect with other people. Miriam looked down that Nile River, saw where Moses was headed and realized he was headed to the Palace. That meant, Miriam needed to connect with someone in the palace make sure her brother would have his needs met. The daughter of Pharaoh had the economic and social capital such that she could ensure Moses' flourishing. There needed to be a connection and relationship between women of different social classes in order for the vulnerable child Moses to survive and thrive.

Miriam sees Moses headed to the home of a woman of means, and asks, "can I help you out with that baby your maid just got out of the river? I can hear Miriam saying, "let me find his mama." There developed a sort of partnership between the women in Moses family and the daughter of Pharaoh. Sometimes, in order to do the most good, in order to address social and economic injustice we need to partner with people who we don't agree with politically or even theologically. Pharaoh's daughter was a wealthy woman of unimaginable means and she was a woman with compassion. She was a woman who didn't go into the river herself, but had a maid working for her who she could recruit to do what needed to be done.

To create a world where the most vulnerable are safe, cared for and can flourish, we need to recruit badass women of means who are unafraid to leverage their privilege on behalf of people outside their country club. The daughter of Pharaoh, a wealthy woman willing to take action and resist the edict of her own father to destroy innocent life. We need to figure out where those women are and recruit them to join us in creating a world where justice rolls down like and every flowing stream; where all God's children have everything, we need to be our best and most authentic selves.

It really does take a village to create this kind of world—the world that I'm convinced God wants. Shiphrah, Puah, Jocabed, Miriam, the daughter of Pharaoh, and her maid, were all participants in Moses' salvation. The courageous acts of these women made it possible for his survival and subsequent thriving as the quintessential prophet and deliverer of God's people. Their unified stories show us the power of collective action as a response to social and civil injustice. If it wasn't for those six badass women there would be no Moses.

Lord, may we be Badass women. *B*

# About the Author

Reverend Dr. Irie Lynne Session, an ordained clergywoman in the Christian Church (Disciples of Christ), is Co-Pastor of The Gathering, A Womanist Church, a new church plant going into its 3rd year in Dallas, Texas. She's a professor in Perkins School of Theology's Course of Study School and an adjunct instructor for Brite Divinity School's Thriving in Ministry program. Dr. Irie holds a Master of Divinity with Certificate in Black Church Studies from Brite Divinity School; and a Doctor of Ministry in Transformative Leadership and Prophetic Preaching from Colgate Rochester Crozer Divinity School.

Dr. Irie spent 17 years in Social Work as a Parole Officer, and as an Investigator for Child Protective Services. She worked in the nonprofit sector for 22 years, dedicating 14 ½ of those years helping transform the lives of survivors of prostitution and other forms of commercial sexual exploitation with New Friends New Life, a Dallas nonprofit.

Now, as a passionate innovator, award winning minister, TEDx Presenter, and Spiritual Entrepreneur, Dr. Irie leverages 30-plus years of social work and ministry as Founder and Chief Illuminator of DreamBig, a ministry addressing economic inequities experienced by clergywomen, women in ministry, women of a certain age, and women of color in church and society by helping them leverage their experience and expertise to make a living for themselves by doing what they're wired to do, and to make a transformative difference in the world.

Dr. Irie is the single mother of India Liana, a freelance make-up artist and budding social media style influencer.

Connect with Dr. Irie on these social media outlets:

**Instagram** - revdririe
**Instagram** - dreambigwithdririe
**Facebook** - revdririe
**Twitter** - @revdririe